NINTH AND TENTH AMENDMENTS: THE RIGHT TO MORE RIGHTS

BY RICH SMITH

SERIES CONSULTANT: SCOTT HARR, J.D. CRIMINAL JUSTICE
DEPARTMENT CHAIR, CONCORDIA UNIVERSITY ST. PAUL

Visit us at
www.abdopublishing.com

Published by ABDO Publishing Company, 8000 West 78th Street, Suite 310, Edina, MN 55439.
Copyright ©2008 by Abdo Consulting Group, Inc. International copyrights reserved in all countries.
No part of this book may be reproduced in any form without written permission from the publisher.
Abdo & Daughters™ is a trademark and logo of ABDO Publishing Company.

Printed in the United States.

Editor: John Hamilton
Graphic Design: Sue Hamilton
Cover Design: Neil Klinepier
Cover Illustration: Getty Images
Interior Photos and Illustrations: p 1 Constitution & flag, iStockphoto; p 5 Constitution & flag, iStockphoto; p 7 Bill of Rights & magnifying glass, iStockphoto; p 8 (top) Bill of Rights, courtesy National Archives, (bottom) Patrick Henry, by George Bagby Matthews, courtesy United States Senate; p 9 (top) Alexander Hamilton, Corbis, (bottom) James Madison, Corbis; p 10 solar eclipse, Getty Images; p 11 Supreme Court, iStockphoto; p 13 Gary & Jenifer Troxel, AP Images; p 15 Minnesota State Capitol building, iStockphoto; p 16 dollar graphic, iStockphoto; p 17 sobriety test, iStockphoto; p 19 radioactive waste containers, iStockphoto; p 21 Civil War reenactor, AP Images; p 23 Great Depression food line, AP Images; p 24 President Franklin D. Roosevelt, Corbis; p 25 FDR at CCC camp, Corbis; p 27 hand holding wheat, iStockphoto; p 28 visitors viewing Constitution at National Archives, Corbis; p 29 bronze plaque of Bill of Rights, Corbis.

Library of Congress Cataloging-in-Publication Data

Smith, Rich, 1954-
  Ninth and tenth amendments : the right to more rights / Rich Smith.
    p. cm. -- (The Bill of Rights)
  Includes index.
  ISBN 978-1-59928-921-2
  1. United States. Constitution 9th Amendment--Juvenile literature. 2. United States. Constitution 10th Amendment--Juvenile literature. 3. Constituent power--United States--Juvenile literature. 4. Federal government--United States--Juvenile literature. 5. State rights--United States--Juvenile literature. I. Title.

  KF4557.S645 2008
  342.73'042--dc22
                    2007014580

CONTENTS

THE NINTH AMENDMENT

Friday night. You've got big plans for a fun evening. But, naturally, the grown-ups in your life want to know about those plans. They throw a barrage of questions at you: "Where are you going? Who are you going with? What will you be doing? What time will you be home?"

You choose to answer like this: "My plan for tonight includes going to the movie theater and then hanging out with my friends at the mall. I figure I'll be home sometime around 11:00 P.M."

Your parents tell you that they have no problem with your plan. Still, they can't resist giving you the usual lecture about staying out of trouble. Then, out the door you go.

Your first stop is the movie theater. From there, you're off to the mall to hang out with friends, just like you said. But it's only 9:30 P.M. The night is still young. Your friends mention that they know of a party at another friend's house. A live band will be playing there. Your friends want to go to that party. They want you to come along. You need no convincing. "Let's rock 'n' roll!" you tell your friends.

The party turns out to be a major event. You have the best time ever, and because of that you completely lose track of the time. The next thing you know, it's 11:45 P.M. You tell your friends you've got to get home. By the time you arrive, the clock says it's midnight. You try sneaking quietly past your parents' room, but somehow they hear you. They rush out, so angry you can almost see smoke coming out of their ears.

"You said you were going to be home at 11:00 P.M. You lied to us," they yell.

You calmly reply to your parents, "I didn't say I would be home *at* 11:00 P.M. I said I would be home *sometime around* 11:00 P.M. I know that it's midnight. That's sometime around 11:00 P.M., just like 10:00 P.M. is sometime around 11:00 P.M."

Above: The Ninth Amendment to the United States Constitution was written to calm fears that naming some rights, but not all, in the Bill of Rights might lead to the government claiming more power than the Founding Fathers intended.

Your parents are even angrier now. They realize they can't punish you for lying about the time you planned to be home because you hadn't stated an exact time to begin with. Ah, but what about where you've been? Your parents received a phone call from one of *their* friends who happens to live right next door to the big party you attended. Their friend saw you there and called your parents, who now accuse you of lying about where you planned to go. "You said you were only going to the movie theater and the mall," they bellow. "We gave our OK because we thought those were the only places you were going."

But you stay calm. You say to your parents, "I didn't say I was *only* going to the movie theater and the mall. I said my plans *included* those two places. By using the word *included*, that meant I would go to those two places but that there might be other places I would go in addition to those two. I didn't list the party in the places I would go because I didn't even know about the party until after I left here at the beginning of the night. So you can't say I lied or tricked you. I was totally truthful."

Your parents look at each other in stunned silence. They know they're beaten. They turn and slowly slink back into their room, quietly shutting the door behind them.

Congratulations! You have successfully explained to a pair of adults the idea behind the Ninth Amendment of the U.S. Constitution.

The Ninth Amendment declares the following: "The enumeration in the Constitution, of certain rights, shall not be construed to deny or disparage others retained by the people."

You're probably scratching your head right about now. You ask yourself, "What does any of that have to do with the example of me not giving my parents a full list of places I planned to go on a Friday night?" It's very simple: The Ninth Amendment basically says that you have a right to more rights than just those that are listed in the First through Eighth Amendments. Those additional rights might not be spelled out, but that doesn't mean they don't exist. The Ninth Amendment assumes they do indeed exist. They just happen to be extra rights that aren't yet known. That's exactly like you not knowing about the Friday night party until after you had already listed off for your parents some but not all of the places you planned to go.

Above: The Ninth Amendment declares that Americans have more rights than those found in the Bill of Rights. Those additional rights might not be spelled out, but that doesn't mean they don't exist.

LET THERE BE LIGHT

Left: The Bill of Rights is stored in the National Archives building in Washington, D.C.

The Ninth Amendment was put into the Bill of Rights because some of the Founding Fathers of the United States were afraid that government would think the only rights people had were the ones listed. There was a big fight among the Founding Fathers about this. Here is how the arguing might have sounded:

Patrick Henry

Founding Father Patrick Henry:

"Give me liberty, or give me death. And while you're at it, give me a Bill of Rights, too. We're going to be entrusting an awful lot of power to the government. We need to have extra protections to make sure government does not try to unjustly increase the power we give it."

Founding Father Alexander Hamilton:

"OK, fine. But you know that First Amendment your side is proposing? It guarantees the right to freedom of speech. But what about the freedom to dance? What about the freedom to paint a work of art? I don't see those freedoms in the First Amendment. And aren't those sort of like speech in a way? The one thing they all have in common is they're forms of expression.

"But your proposed First Amendment doesn't specifically guarantee a right to freedom of expression. If the government decides to one day pass a law forbidding dancing and painting, you won't be able to claim that such a law is a violation of the First Amendment. You won't be able to make that claim because freedom of expression and freedom to dance and freedom to paint are not listed among the rights of the First Amendment."

Founding Father
James Madison:
"Well, Al, you've got a point there. And so do you, Pat. Let's see if we can solve this problem by including in the Bill of Rights a Ninth Amendment. That way, we can be sure to cover all our bases. We can list the freedoms we consider most important without anyone in the future making the mistake of thinking they're the only ones."

Madison was the Founding Father who did most of the writing of the Constitution. He was also in charge of putting together the Bill of Rights. Madison wanted it understood that the rights not listed in the Bill of Rights were not rights that would have to be invented. Instead, they were rights that already existed. All that needed to happen was for them to be discovered. And the way they would be discovered was by taking a close look at human nature.

Alexander Hamilton

James Madison

Above: During a solar eclipse, the Moon passes between Earth and the Sun. The light from the Sun is blocked out, except for a narrow band of glowing light called a penumbra.

That's what the justices of the United States Supreme Court did in 1965. They were considering a case called *Griswold v. Connecticut.* The justices realized that four of the amendments in the Bill of Rights point to an undiscovered right. That right was the right to privacy.

There were two important words used by the justices in discovering the right to privacy. The first word was *penumbra.* A penumbra is something that happens during a total eclipse of the Sun. During an eclipse, the Moon passes between Earth and the Sun. That makes it appear as if the Sun is going dark. At the height of the eclipse, the Sun is entirely blocked out, except for a narrow band of glowing light along its outer edge. That small area of light is called the penumbra.

The second word used by the Supreme Court was *emanation.* An emanation is anything that comes from or flows out of something else. For example, light comes from the Sun. You could then say that light is an emanation of the Sun. Likewise, the right to privacy is an emanation of other rights in the Bill of Rights. Specifically, the justices of the Supreme Court said the right to privacy can't normally be seen in the Constitution because the light emanating from the First, Third, Fourth, and Fifth Amendments is so bright. Yet that light is what creates a penumbra in each of those rights. It is within those penumbras that extra rights exist and can be found. All you need do in order to see the penumbras is temporarily block the light of the amendments.

Above: The United States Supreme Court building in Washington, D.C.

POWER TO THE PEOPLE

Another right not listed in the Bill of Rights but which can be found by studying human nature is the right of parents to decide how best to raise their own children. This right was at the heart of a 2000 case known as *Troxel v. Granville*.

The case began in the state of Washington. A woman by the name of Tommie Granville had two young daughters. The girls' father was a man by the name of Brad Troxel. Ms. Granville and Mr. Troxel never married, and later went their separate ways. After that, Mr. Troxel lived with his parents. However, every weekend he picked up his daughters from their mother's house and brought them for a two-day stay at his parents' home. Things continued like this for the next two years. Then, Mr. Troxel died. His parents, Gary and Jenifer Troxel, wanted the girls to keep coming for visits every weekend, just as before. But Ms. Granville felt the girls should only visit the Troxels for a single day, once a month.

The Troxels became angry, and went to court and asked a judge to order Ms. Granville to give them the grandchildren every weekend. The Troxels could make such a request in court because Washington had a law allowing anybody to ask for visitation rights. The request could come from a family member, a friend, or even a perfect stranger. The point was that it would be up to the court to decide who could visit a child and on what days.

The superior court judge who heard the case granted the Troxels' request. He ordered Ms. Granville to let the Troxels have the girls every weekend. Ms. Granville appealed the order. Through her attorney, she argued that Washington's law was unconstitutional because it violated her basic human right to raise her own children and make decisions for them. The appeals court agreed with Ms. Granville. So did the state supreme court and the United States Supreme Court.

The justices of the U.S. Supreme Court found that the Constitution allows the government to interfere with a parent's right to raise his or her own child only if the child is in some kind of danger. However, not all of the justices agreed with this ruling. A few felt this decision gave permission for using the Ninth Amendment to invent new rights rather than merely discover ones that already exist. Justice Antonin Scalia started out by saying that the right of parents to direct the upbringing of their children is an unalienable right and one that the Ninth Amendment should protect. But then he went on to say that the proper way for this and all other undiscovered rights to be discovered is through Congress, not the courts. The reason he said this is because of his belief that the House of Representatives and the Senate are the voice of the people. And that is who the Ninth Amendment was written for—the people.

Above: Gary and Jenifer Troxel at the United States Supreme Court in Washington, D.C., January 12, 2000.

THE TENTH AMENDMENT

Years ago, older teenagers in many states could legally drink alcohol. They did not have to be 21 years old before they could buy beer and other adult beverages. They only had to be 18 or 19 years old.

Then, in 1984, Congress passed a law called the National Minimum Drinking Age Act. This federal law did not order the states to raise their legal age for drinking to 21. It only "offered" that they do so. But as offers went, this was one the states found they couldn't refuse.

The federal law said that any state failing to raise its drinking age to 21 would lose out on money from Congress to build and maintain highways. A state that defied the federal government might lose many millions of dollars. And without that money, a state might not be able to fix the potholes in its roads. Or it might not be able to widen its highways in places where traffic jams always seem to happen. It might not be able to keep its bridges in good repair, or do any of a thousand different things to help make travel by car, bus, truck, or motorcycle safer for everyone.

One by one, the states agreed to raise their minimum drinking age. All except South Dakota, which sued in federal court to have the National Minimum Drinking Age Act thrown out. South Dakota said it was an unconstitutional law. The state asked the court to rule that the law violated the Tenth Amendment, the final amendment of the Bill of Rights.

Here are the words of the Tenth Amendment: "The powers not delegated to the United States by the Constitution, nor prohibited by it to the States, are reserved for the States respectively, or to the people."

Above: The Minnesota State Capitol, located in St. Paul, Minnesota. The Tenth Amendment of the United States Constitution reminds the federal government that some powers are reserved for the states and for the people.

Right: To receive federal money for their highways, states must enforce the National Minimum Drinking Age Act, which declares that people cannot legally drink alcohol until the age of 21.

In simpler language, this means that the federal government cannot boss the states, unless the Constitution says so. South Dakota did not believe the Constitution said anything about the federal government being able to threaten the states in this manner if they did not obey commands from the nation's capital.

The district court did not agree with South Dakota. The court said the federal government did indeed have such power. That power is found in the part of the Constitution that talks about Congress being able to spend money as it sees fit. That part is Article I, Section 8, Clause 1.

South Dakota was unwilling to accept the district court's ruling, so it appealed. But the appeals court also ruled against South Dakota. The state appealed once more, this time to the United States Supreme Court. Things went no better for South Dakota there either.

In its 1987 ruling in the case of *South Dakota v. Dole*, the High Court upheld the decisions of the federal district court and the appeals court. No violation of the Tenth Amendment had occurred. The Supreme Court told South Dakota that if allowing older teenagers to drink was so important, all the state had to do was just say no to the federal government's offer of highway money. The Court said that nobody was forcing South Dakota to take the money. As a result, the Court found it perfectly constitutional for Congress to hold back money promised to a state until that state agreed to cooperate with federal law.

Above: A driver is stopped and given a sobriety test.

A GREENISH GLOW

Five years after *South Dakota v. Dole,* a somewhat similar case reached the Supreme Court. However, this time the ruling went against the federal government because the Tenth Amendment had been violated. The case was *New York v. United States* (1992).

This legal battle began in 1985 when Congress passed and the president signed into law a bill known as the Low-Level Radioactive Waste Policy Amendments Act. Radioactive waste of all types had grown to be a very serious issue for the nation. High-level radioactive wastes are the most dangerous kind. They include things like used-up uranium fuel rods at atomic power plants, where electricity is made. Low-level radioactive wastes are less dangerous. They include things like leftover isotopes from nuclear medicines and X-ray equipment, along with contaminated radiation suits and hoods. All of this waste has to go somewhere, and the federal government in 1985 wanted to make sure that wherever it ended up it would not harm people or the environment.

The Low-Level Radioactive Waste Policy Amendments Act worked in some ways like the National Minimum Drinking Age Act. Congress told the states what it wanted done, and then threatened to hold back promised cash if the states didn't obey. But then Congress made the mistake of also telling the states that they alone would be responsible for paying money awarded by the courts to the victims of low-level radioactive wastes that had been under federal government control.

The state of New York thought this was unfair. So New York went to court against the federal government to block this new law. The case worked its way up to the United States Supreme Court. The High Court said Congress this time had indeed gone too far. The justices ruled that the federal government couldn't just go around snapping its fingers and ordering the states to do what it wants. That is a violation of what are referred to as *states' rights.*

Yes, it's true: states have rights, just like people. And that's what the Tenth Amendment is meant to protect, the rights of the states. But the Tenth Amendment also is meant to protect the rights of the people. All the people. Not just individuals, which is who the first eight amendments are meant to protect.

In the United States, the power to make laws and do other important work on behalf of the people starts with the states. However, each state has agreed to give up some of that power. The power given up has been placed in the hands of a central government. The powers given to the central government are all spelled out in the Constitution.

This type of government system is called federalism. Under federalism, the most important powers are held by the central government. It has to be that way in order for the central government to carry out its mission of protecting the nation, promoting progress, and seeing to it that prosperity spreads far and wide.

Above: Radioactive waste containers. Part of the federal government's Low-Level Radioactive Waste Policy Amendments Act was ruled unconstitutional because the law violated the Tenth Amendment.

MAKING A FEDERAL CASE OUT OF IT

FEDERALISM WAS NOT the system of government used by the United States in the first 20 or so years after the country began. Instead, the country used something similar called a confederative system. As a confederation, the states held far more power than the central government. For example, the central government at that time had no power to make anyone pay taxes.

The nation changed to federalism when it adopted the Constitution. From that time on, laws created by Congress had priority over similar laws passed by the states. This is a rule known as the Supremacy Clause, which is spelled out in Article VI of the Constitution.

Here is an example of how that works: Pretend your state has a law requiring you to drink milk once per day. But the central government has a law requiring you to drink milk three times per day. Those are similar laws that both require the drinking of milk every day. Yet they are different because one law requires milk drinking more times per day than the other. Which law should you obey? The Supremacy Clause of the Constitution settles that question for you. The federal law is the one you obey because it is a higher law than the state law.

Some of the Framers of the Constitution worried that the Supremacy Clause would allow Congress to pass so many laws similar to state laws that eventually only federal law would count in every situation. That was one of the reasons the Framers insisted that the Tenth Amendment be included in the Bill of Rights. They wanted a way to prevent the central government from becoming too strong.

The Tenth Amendment is a good thing, except when it is used for a wrong purpose. Take the Civil War, for example. The Civil War started because the states of the South were in favor of slavery. The states of the North were against it. The Northern states kept pushing the federal government to get rid of slavery. The Southern states said slavery could not be banned by the federal government because of the Tenth Amendment.

Above: A Civil War reenactor portrays an African-American Union soldier.

They said that the issue of slavery was a matter to be decided at the state level of government. The South warned that if the Tenth Amendment were violated, they would drop out of the United States and form their own country. This new country would be much like the United States before the Constitution came along. It would be a confederation of states in which the federal government had only a small amount of power compared to the power of each state. The South eventually did leave the United States, but was brought back in after it lost the Civil War in 1865.

Do Desperate Times Call for Desperate Measures?

The Tenth Amendment makes it clear that the powers not specifically granted to the central government are to remain in the hands of the states or of the people. Many important tests of this guarantee occurred during the Great Depression of the 1930s. The Great Depression was a time when the economy of the United States suffered an enormous blow. It started with the stock market crash of 1929. The crash caused a large number of businesses to fail because their stocks became worthless. As a result, many people lost their jobs or saw their entire life's savings wiped out. It became difficult and sometimes impossible to buy or sell even the most basic things like food and clothes. The misery of the Great Depression was at its worst in 1933. Life slowly returned to normal after that, but it was not until the United States entered World War II in 1941 that the Great Depression completely ended.

When the Great Depression began, the federal government tried to bring it to a quick stop. But there was only so much the government could do without violating the Constitution and the Tenth Amendment. One way the government tried to fight the Great Depression was by keeping foreign-made products from entering the country. Government leaders thought the American economy would be strengthened if businesses were protected from overseas competition. However, this did not work as planned.

Above: Hundreds of jobless men line up for a free dinner outside New York City's municipal lodging house in the winter of 1932-33 during the Great Depression.

Above: President Franklin Delano Roosevelt.

By this point, the people were becoming desperate. Many wanted the government to take action using powers not allowed by the Constitution. In 1932, Franklin D. Roosevelt was elected president of the United States. He believed that sometimes it's necessary to go against the rules if it's for an important enough reason, and rescuing the nation from financial ruin was just such an important reason.

Roosevelt came up with a plan to repair the damage caused by the Great Depression. He called this plan the "New Deal." It included having the federal government create jobs paid for with tax dollars to get people back to work. It also included programs to change the way that many kinds of businesses operate. Some of these programs helped the nation start moving again. Even so, quite a few people worried that the power of the federal government was growing and getting way out of control. Opponents of Roosevelt's New Deal believed the Framers of the Constitution would spin in their graves if they could see just how far outside the limits government had gone.

Anti-New Dealers sued the government to stop President Roosevelt. Their lawsuits reached the Supreme Court, where they often won. The High Court ruled that many of the New Deal programs were violations of the Constitution and the Tenth Amendment.

But then a strange thing happened. The president proposed increasing the size of the Supreme Court from 9 justices to 15. That would allow him to appoint to the Supreme Court six more justices. Each of those new justices would be a good friend of his, sharing Roosevelt's views about government power. There would then be enough justices in favor of the New Deal to make further wins by the anti-New Dealers unlikely.

Above: As part of his New Deal, President Franklin D. Roosevelt (in the car, next to the cake) visits a Civilian Conservation Corps (CCC) camp in Bear Mountain State Park, New York, in 1933.

Congress rejected the idea of adding more justices to the Supreme Court. However, the very fact that Roosevelt had proposed such a plan frightened some Supreme Court justices. They started changing their minds about the Tenth Amendment and the Constitution's limits on federal power. They soon afterward came out with rulings more to the liking of the president. And with that came many big jumps in the size and authority of the federal government.

One of these cases was *Wickard v. Filburn* (1942). Wheat farmer Roscoe Filburn was accused of breaking a New Deal law called the Agricultural Adjustment Act of 1938. This law was meant to steady the price of wheat. During the Great Depression, wheat prices fell so low that many farmers did not find it worth the effort and expense to raise the crop. The Agricultural Adjustment Act worked by telling farmers exactly how much wheat to grow on each acre of land they owned. Farmer Filburn broke the law by growing more wheat than he was allowed. In court, he said the extra wheat was not going to be sold. The extra wheat was only to feed himself and his family. He also tried to have the charges against him thrown out on the grounds that the federal government had no constitutional right to create such a law in the first place.

The federal government fired back that it did have the right. It pointed to the Constitution's Commerce Clause, which is found in Article I, Section 8. The Commerce Clause gives the federal government power to tell companies how they must conduct business when they buy or sell products in states other than the one where they are headquartered. Farmer Filburn wondered how the Commerce Clause could matter in his situation, since the extra wheat he raised was not shipped to another state and never even left his property.

The Supreme Court answered by saying that Filburn's wheat for his personal use did in fact have something to do with the Commerce Clause. The Court explained that if he had not grown the additional wheat, Filburn would then have been forced to buy it from the grocery store. But by not buying from the grocery store, Filburn was having an effect on the grocery store's business. And it wasn't only the grocery store that was affected by Filburn not shopping there. Also affected were all the companies involved in providing goods and services to the grocery store. Affected too were all the companies doing business with all the companies supporting the grocery store where Filburn was not shopping.

The High Court reasoned that many of those affected companies would almost surely be located in another state. As a result, the Commerce Clause applied, and no violation of the Constitution or the Tenth Amendment had occurred, the Supreme Court ruled.

Above: When wheat farmer Roscoe Filburn was accused of breaking a New Deal law, he fought the charges all the way to the Supreme Court in the 1942 case of *Wickard v. Filburn*. The Court decided that the Tenth Amendment had not been violated.

CONCLUSION

The case of *Wickard v. Filburn* is a good example of how the rights guaranteed by the Constitution's Bill of Rights are not absolute. If they were absolute, farmer Filburn would never have gotten into the trouble he found himself in. Instead, as this case shows, the rights listed in the Bill of Rights are limited. Limiting the rights of the people is necessary in order for the government to keep the public safe and keep the streets peaceful.

The trick is in making sure that there is a proper balance between the rights of individuals and the responsibilities of government. Sometimes the balance shifts too much in one direction at the expense of the other. But in the end, the right balance will be found. It always is. That's because the American Constitution and its Bill of Rights are sturdy enough and flexible enough for the job.

Facing page: A candle illuminates a bronze plaque of the Bill of Rights.
Right: Visitors gaze at the Constitution and the Declaration of Independence on exhibit in the National Archives building in Washington, D.C. Sealed in bronze and glass cases filled with helium, the precious parchments can be lowered at a moment's notice into a large fireproof and shockproof vault.

The Bill of Rig...

Amendment I

...pecting an establishment of religion, or prohibiting the free e...
...t of the people peaceably to assemble, and to petition the Gove...

Amendment II

...essary to the security of a free State, the right of the people to kee...

Amendment III

...e be quartered in any house, without the consent of the Owner, n...

Amendment IV

...ure in their persons, houses, papers, and effects, against unreasonab...
...e, But upon probable cause, supported by Oath or affirmation, a...
...gs to be seized.

Amendment V

...for a capital, or otherwise infamous crime, unless on a present...
...naval forces, or in the Militia, when in actual service in time of...
...ce to be twice put in jeopardy of life or limb; nor shall be co...
...ved of life, liberty, or property, without due process of law; no...

Amendment VI

...used shall enjoy the right to a speedy and public trial, by an imp...
...mmitted, which district shall have been previously ascertained...
...be confronted with the witnesses against him; to have compulsor...
...f Counsel for his defence.

Amendment VII

...alue in controversy shall exceed twenty dollars, the right of trial...
...e-examined in any Court of the United States, than according to...

Amendment VIII

...or excessive fines imposed, nor cruel and unusual punishments in...

Amendment IX

...f certain rights, shall not be construed to deny or disparage oth...

Amendment X

...red States by the Constitution, nor proh...

GLOSSARY

AMENDMENT

When it was created, the Constitution wasn't perfect. The Founding Fathers wisely added a special section. It allowed the Constitution to be changed by future generations. This makes the Constitution flexible. It is able to bend to the will of the people it governs. Changes to the Constitution are called amendments. The first 10 amendments are called the Bill of Rights. An amendment must be approved by two-thirds of both houses of Congress. Once that happens, the amendment must be approved by three-fourths of the states. Then it becomes law. This is a very difficult thing to do. The Framers of the Constitution didn't want it changed unless there was a good reason. There have been over 9,000 amendments proposed. Only 27 of them have been ratified, or made into law. Some amendments changed the way our government works. The Twelfth Amendment changed the way we elect our president. The Twenty-Second Amendment limits a president to two terms in office. Constitutional amendments have also increased the freedoms of our citizens. The Thirteenth Amendment finally got rid of slavery. And the Nineteenth Amendment gave women the right to vote.

BILL OF RIGHTS

The first 10 amendments to the United States Constitution make up what is known as the Bill of Rights. The Bill of Rights lists the special freedoms every human is born with and is able to enjoy in America. Also, the Bill of Rights tells the government that it cannot stop people from fully using and enjoying those freedoms unless the government has an extremely good reason for doing so.

CONFEDERATION

A nation comprised of individual states that are loosely united. The most important powers are reserved for the states, which are held together by a weak central government.

FEDERALISM

A type of government with individual states bound together by a strong central authority. The central government is given power to protect the nation and promote progress and prosperity. The United States today is a federalist nation.

Founding Fathers

The men who participated in the Constitutional Convention in 1787, especially the ones who signed the Constitution. Some of the Founding Fathers included George Washington, Benjamin Franklin, John Rutledge, Gouverneur Morris, Alexander Hamilton, and James Madison.

Great Depression

A time of worldwide economic hardship that began in 1929 and lasted through most of the 1930s. Millions of people lost jobs or were made homeless during the Depression.

High Court

Another name for the United States Supreme Court.

Lawsuit

A legal way to settle a dispute in which both sides argue their case in front of a judge or jury in a court of law. The person who has been wronged is called the plaintiff. The person being sued is called the defendant. Plaintiffs and defendants can be individuals, or they can be businesses or government entities, such as corporations or towns. People can even sue the United States, which is how many cases are filed involving the Constitution and violation of rights.

Sue

To bring a lawsuit against a person or institution in a court of law.

Supreme Court

The United States Supreme Court is the highest court in the country. There are nine judges on the Supreme Court. They make sure local, state, and federal governments are following the rules spelled out in the United States Constitution. Our understanding of the Constitution evolves over time. It is up to the Supreme Court to decide how the Constitution is applied to today's society. When the Supreme Court rules on a case, other courts in the country must follow the decision in similar situations. In this way, the laws of the Constitution are applied equally to all Americans.

INDEX